THE LIFE CYCLE
WORKBOOK
By Joel Lurie Grishaver

alternatives in religious education, inc.

Published by:
A.R.E. Publishing, Inc.
an Imprint of Behrman House, Inc.
Springfield, New Jersey

ISBN 10: 0-86705-135-3
ISBN 13: 978-0-86705-135-3

NOTES FOR TEACHERS

The Life Cycle Workbook presents a way of looking at important moments in a Jew's life. The book can be used independently or in conjunction with existing text materials. While the age level is defined as Intermediate, or Grades 4-6, the workbook will be of use for older learners as well, even including adults.

The book is divided into six modules: LIFE CYCLES — the concept of a life cycle; BIRTH EVENTS; TORAH EVENTS — includes consecration, Bar/Bat Mitzvah and Confirmation; WEDDINGS/MARRIAGE; DEATH/MOURNING. In addition, there is a REVIEW MODULE.

For each module there are several basic types of sheets: a Content Overview, a Vocabulary Sheet, a Vocabulary Worksheet, a Primary Jewish Text to study, a Text Worksheet, a Parent Interview (students discuss major events in the life cycle with their parents) and a Values Exercise which enables the students to personalize the subject matter. Some modules have additional worksheets besides those mentioned above, and not every kind of worksheet has been included for every module.

The chart below indicates which worksheets are provided for each of the six modules and the page number on which each may be found.

	CONTENT OVERVIEW	VOCAB. SHEET	VOCAB. DRILL	TEXT	TEXT STUDY SHEET	PARENT INTERVIEW	VALUES PIECE	EXTRA WORK-SHEET
LIFE CYCLE	5	7		8	9	10-11	12-13	6
BIRTH	14-15	16-17	21	18-19	20	24-25	22-23	
TORAH	26-27	28	29	30		31-32	33	
MARRIAGE	34-35	36	37	38-39	40	41		
DEATH	42-43 48			44		46	47	45
REVIEW	49				50		52	51

A cycle is something that goes **round**.
A cycle is something that happens
over and **over** again.

Bicycles have two things that
go **round**.
Summer-Winter-Fall-Spring is a **cycle**.
The moon has a **cycle**.
And, even years come **around**.

(On the back of this page, list as many cycles as you can.)

BUT HOW DOES A LIFE CYCLE?

It's hard to talk about **life cycles**. We are all born...
We will all die (someday). It seems like we live a

LIFE LINE

BIRTH ————————————————→ DEATH

We can mark off all kinds of events along our **life line**.

BIRTH ——— 1st Grade ——— Bar/Bat Mitzvah ——— Graduate High School ——— Marriage ————————————————→ DEATH

One of those events can be the
birth of another person. That starts a second
line. If we look at the way certain events
happen over and over, how they happen to everyone, we can see that

LIVES ARE CYCLES.

The special events, the landmarks, the things that
happen over and over, become special moments. We Jews

 some of these moments.

LIST AS MANY KINDS OF CYCLES AS YOU CAN:

_____

_____

_____

_____

_____

_____

_____

_____

_____

_____

_____

_____

_____

_____

_____

_____

_____

_____

_____

_____

_____

_____

_____

_____

_____

LIFE·CYCLE

"Even as one is entered into the Brit, so may one be entered into Torah, Chuppah and good deeds."

Brit Milah – Entering an eight-day old son into the covenant through circumcision

Brit Banot – A covenant ceremony for girls

Naming – A ceremony when names are given

Pidyon-Haben – Redeeming a firstborn son

K'dushat Pehter Rechem – A new ceremony which redeems any firstborn child

Ben Torah – A "son of the Torah" (When a boy starts to study, he becomes one.)

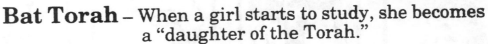

Bat Torah – When a girl starts to study, she becomes a "daughter of the Torah."

Consecration – Ceremony for first year religious school kids

Bar Mitzvah – At 13, a boy becomes a Bar Mitzvah.

Bat Mitzvah – At 13, a girl becomes a Bat Mitzvah.

Confirmation – A ceremony for 9th or 10th graders

Aufruf – A celebration on the Shabbat before the wedding

Erusin/Kiddushin – Engagement

Nissuin – Marriage

Chupah – Bridal canopy (to get married under)

Ketubah – Wedding contract

Get – A divorce (not a necessary part of marriage)

Keriah – Tearing of clothes (or a ribbon)

Kaddish – A prayer, said by mourners

Shiva – First seven days of mourning

Shanah – A year (11 month) mourning period

Sheloshim – 30 day mourning period

Yahrzeit – Anniversary of death

Yizkor – A memorial service held on major Jewish holidays

PIRKE AVOT 5:24

At 5 one is ready to study Torah.

At 10 one is ready to study Mishnah.

At 13 one is ready to observe the Mitzvot.

At 15 one is ready to study Talmud.

At 18 one is ready for marriage.

At 20 one is ready to earn a living.

at 30 one is at the peak of strength.

At 40 one is ready for widsom.

At 50 one is ready to give counsel.

At 60 old age creeps in.

At 70, fullness of years.

At 80, the age of strength.

At 90 the body is bent.

At 100 one is as good as dead.

This is the lifetime of a person as seen by the Rabbis more than 2,000 years ago.

QUESTIONS:

What do children do? _____

What do adults do? _____

What is old age like? _____

How does your life differ from someone older than you? _____

_____

WRITE & DRAW YOUR OWN AGES OF PEOPLE:

AT 5	AT 10	AT 13	AT 15
AT 18	AT 20	AT 30	AT 40
AT 50	AT 60	AT 70	AT 80
AT 90	AT 100		

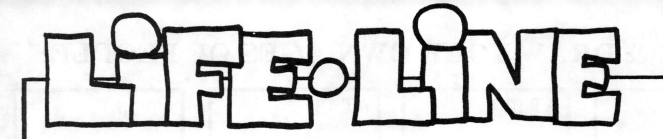

LIFE·LINE

We've talked about life lines. Now interview a few people (maybe your parents) and then fill in their life lines. Use the questions below to help.

Name _____

BIRTH

Name _____

BIRTH

QUESTIONS TO ASK . . .

List the 5 most important moments of your life.
List the 3 happiest moments.
List the 3 saddest moments.
List 2 of the most embarrassing moments.
Add your own questions and record the information on the
life lines.

FILL IN YOUR LIFE GAME

On the game board, fill in 2 of the most important things that have happened to you, and 3 things that you hope will happen.

Fill in 2 important Jewish events that have happened to you, and 2 which you hope will happen.

Put in 5 happy events.
Put in 3 serious events.
Put in 3 silly events.

Use your imagination to fill in the rest of the squares.

Invent a game you can play on this board. Name your game and write the rules here.

Name of the game: _____

The rules: _____
_____
_____
_____
_____
_____
_____
_____
_____
_____
_____
_____

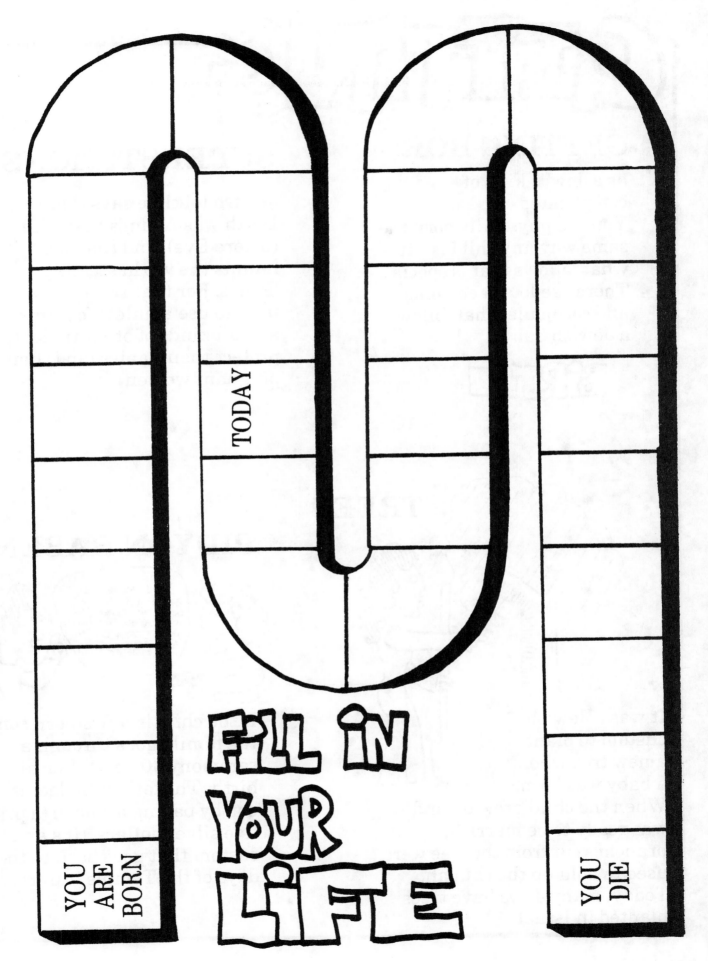

GETTING BORN

as a Jew is kind of complicated.
You are physically born the same way any child is. It is what follows that is special. There are lots of customs and cermonies that follow a Jewish baby's

SUPERSTITIONS

Jewish folklore says that Lilith was Adam's first wife (before Eve), and that she haunts the world stealing babies. For that reason Jews used to use amulets (charms) and all kinds of other tricks to protect their babies (and their pregnant women).

TREES

It was a Jewish custom to plant a new tree when a baby was born. When the child grew up and was ready to be married, branches cut from the tree were used to hold up the chupah. Today, many Jews have trees planted in Israel.

PIDYON HABEN

EVEN AS HE HAS BEEN ENTERED INTO THE REDEMPTION, SO MAY HE BE ENTERED INTO TORAH, CHUPAH AND GOOD DEEDS.

If the child is a firstborn son, the family goes through a ceremony 30 days after his birth. The father "redeems" his son by paying a Kohen (a priest) five silver dollars. (It's an old custom that goes back to the days of the Temple in Jerusalem.)

BRIT MILAH

On the eighth day after birth, the foreskin is removed from the newborn boy's penis. He is entered into the Jewish people, as this covenant is cut. In Hebrew, covenants are "cut" not "made."

SHALOM ZACHAR

CHICK-PEAS

If the baby is a boy, a special party is given on the Friday night before the **Brit Milah.** The Shema and Psalms are read, and chick-peas are eaten.

NAMING

Naming is an important part of this process. A boy is traditionally named at his Brit. A girl traditionally is named in the synagogue on a Shabbat following her birth when her father is called to the Torah.

WIMPEL

In times gone by, a mother often took her child's new diaper and embroidered it as a Torah binder which was then presented to the synagogue.

BIRTH STORY WORD LIST

BRIT – Covenant (of)

MILAH – Circumcision

SHALOM ZACHAR – A special party given on the Friday night before the brit.

SEUDAT MITZVAH – A party given after performing a mitzvah, in this case, right after the Brit Milah.

K'VATER (man)
K'VATERIN (woman)
is the Godfather/Godmother who brings the child into the room.

SANDEK is the person who sits in the chair of Elijah and holds the baby on a pillow during the Brit Milah cermony.

PIDYON – Redeeming

HABEN – The son

SEUDAT MITZVAH – A party given after performing a mitzvah, in this case, right after the Pidyon Haben.

FATHER　　　　**5 SILVER DOLLARS**

"All the firstborn sons you shall redeem." (Exodus 34:20)
"...and their redemption money... shall be...five shekels."
(Numbers 18:15)

Jewish birth rituals were traditionally boy centered. Girls were simply named in synagogue when the father was called to the Torah. Today lots of people are creating new ceremonies for girl babies. **BRIT BANOT** – A covenant ceremony for girls.

MOHEL is the person trained to perform the circumcision (Milah).

KOHEN – Today a Kohen is an ordinary person who is probably named Cohen. Back in the days of the Temple, a Kohen was a priest.

'DUSHAT PEHTER ECHEM – celebration any firstborn child oy or girl).

Draw lines and match the things that go together. An item on either side can match up with <u>more</u> than one item on the other side.

SHALOM ZACHAR •	• **BOY**
	• **GIRL**
BRIT MILAH •	• **SEUDAT MITZVAH**
	• **FATHER**
BRIT BANOT •	• **MOTHER**
	• **MOHEL**
NAMING •	• **KOHEN**
	• **SANDEK**
PIDYON HABEN •	• **5 SILVER DOLLARS**
	• **K'VATER**
K'DUSHAT PEHTER RECHEM •	• **FIRSTBORN**

Invent a new birth custom:

Name of custom: _____

The people involved: _____

_____

What takes place: _____

_____
_____
_____
_____

BRIT Mi·LAH THE TEXT

1. The brit usually takes place on the eighth day following a boy's birth. The K'vater or the K'vaterin brings the child into the room and everyone present (at least a minyan) says, *"Baruch Ha-ba."*

2. The father, wearing a tallit, takes the child and says the first prayer. Then he gives the child to the Mohel.

3. The Mohel takes the child and places him on a pillow on the lap of the Sandek who is sitting on a chair which is called the chair of Elijah. The Mohel then says this prayer.

4. The Mohel says a blessing. The Sandek holds the boy's legs and then the Mohel uses a flawless knife to remove the foreskin of the penis. (This hurts the child very little because his nerves are not yet finely developed.)

5. The father says a blessing (now that the milah or operation part of the service is over).

6. Then the minyan says:

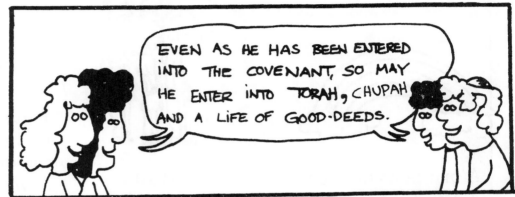

7. Finally, Kiddush is said. Even the child is given a few drops of wine. The boy is then named and everyone goes to the Seudat Mitzvah.

Let's find the key idea in each section: (fill in the blanks)

1. In the first statement, the minyan says _____

2. In the second prayer, the father prepares for the circumcision because it is a _____ .

3. Next, the prophet _____ is mentioned.

4. The Mohel says a blessing over the mitzvah he is about to perform. When God gave us the mitzvot, he _____ us with them.

5. Then the father says the blessing which states that the purpose of this mitzvah is to enter the child into the _____ of Abraham.

6. The minyan then responds with good wishes for the boy's whole
   _____.

7. Finally, we say the _____ which is said at all
   _____ holidays and celebrations.

WRITE DOWN THE NUMBER OF THE BRIT PRAYER WHICH USES EACH OF THESE IDEAS:

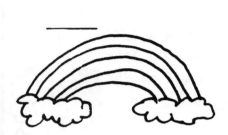

A brit lasts forever.
A covenant should be for
the child's whole life.

A minyan
represents
all of the
Jewish people.

Having a Brit Milah
(being circumcised)
makes a child
Jewish by entering
him into Abraham's
deal (covenant)
with God.

When Elijah
returns, the
world will be
a better place.
(Meanwhile we
do mitzvot.)

A mitzvah is
something you
have to get
ready to do.

Circumcision
is a mitzvah,
something we
are commanded
to do.

Wine is used
to bring joy
and holiness to
every Jewish
ceremony/celebration.

BRIT MILAH

WORKSHEET

ACROSS

2. _____ Milah
3. Performs the Brit
4. Holds the baby
6. Torah, _____ , good deeds
8. _____ of Elijah
9. Godfather
10. The baby is given drops of

12. A prophet
15. the firstborn son is _____
17. _____ born son
18. At a Brit, a boy is _____
19. Mitzvah means ___
20. A covenant ceremony for
    girls is a Brit ___

DOWN

1. Circumcision (Hebrew)
3. Seudat _____
4. A Friday night party for a
   newborn boy _____ _____
5. Godmother
7. _____ Haben
11. Brit Milah is a Jewish
    _____ .
13. The covenant of _____
14. Brit means _____ .
16. Father wears a _____
    at a Brit.

PRINT YOUR WHOLE NAME

Your name is an important part of you. It may even have a lot to do with who you are. The Bible and the Midrash tell this story about how names affect a person. God tells Adam...

Let's take a look at your name.

My first name is

_____ and

I was named after

_____.

Three things I know about the person I was named for are:

(1) _____

(2) _____

(3) _____

Some famous people who share(d) my name are:

_____

_____

_____

_____

My Hebrew name is _____ Ben/Bat

_____ and _____.

It means _____. In Hebrew

I was named after _____.

American Indian names describe what parents would like their children to be. (Running Bear, Quiet Dove, etc.)

If I had an Indian name, I'd pick _____.

Nicknames are the same kind of thing. One of my nicknames is _____.

It means _____.

When I'm called by it I feel _____
_____.

USE THIS SPACE:

Fill it with a creative drawing using your name. It can be a LOGO, a SEAL, a CREST, a COAT of ARMS, or your own idea.

QUESTIONNAIRE

Brit Milah is a covenant cermony. Before we talk more about it in class, ask your parents the following questions:

EVERYONE: What is a brit (bris) for? _____
_____
_____

What is a covenant? _____
_____
_____

BOYS: When, where and by whom (and why) was I circumcised?
_____
_____
_____

How did you make these decisions? _____
_____

If you had it to do over again, would you change anything? _____
_____
_____

GIRLS: What kind of Jewish ceremony was held for me after
I was born? _____
_____
_____

How did you make these decisions? _____
_____
_____

If you had it to do over again, would you change anything?) _____
_____

(Continued on the next page)

GIRLS: When, where, by whom and why was/were my brother(s) circumcised? (If you don't have a brother, ask what would have happened if you did?)

_____

_____

_____

_____

BOYS: What kind of Jewish ceremony was held when my sister(s) was/were born? (If you don't have a sister, ask what would have happened if you did.) _____

_____

_____

_____

EVERYONE: Make up 2 questions of your own and ask them of your parents.

_____

_____

_____

_____

_____

_____

_____

_____

_____

_____

_____

_____

_____

_____

_____

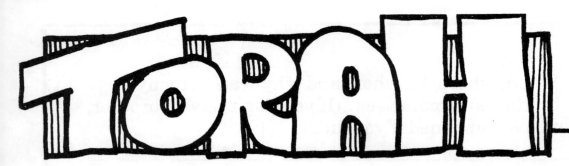

TORAH

תּוֹרָה צִוָּה לָנוּ מֹשֶׁה

When parents began to teach their children to speak, the first thing they would teach them was **TORAH TZIVAH LANU MOSHE**. Moses commanded us to study Torah.

Back in Eastern Europe, parents made a big deal out of the **first day** of school. Mother would bake honey coated letters of the alphabet. Father would **wrap** the child in his **tallit** and **carry** him on his **back** to school.

BAT MITZVAH   BAR MITZVAH

Sometime around his 13th birthday a boy celebrates his becoming a Bar Mitzvah by reading from the Torah. Rabbi Mordecai Kaplan thought it unfair that only boys had such a ceremony. He invented a Bat Mitzvah ceremony for his daughter so that she, too, could enter adulthood with a Jewish religious ceremony.

BAR/BAT MITZVAH

CONSECRATION

Today we have a ceremony called Consecration which celebrates that first school day.

A Bar/Bat Mitzvah is not something you do. It is something you become. At 13 (whether or not you do anything about it) you become a Bar/Bat Mitzvah. The idea is to show the community that a boy/girl is now responsible for the mitzvot. Being called to the Torah is the most important responsibility the Jewish tradition has. Remember, you become a Bar/Bat Mitzvah — you don't have one.

CONFIRMATION

Confirmation is another new ceremony. It was invented by Reform Jews who felt that 13 was too young to mark the final formal point in Jewish education. So Confirmation is a kind of graduation ceremony in 9th or 10th grade. But Confirmation or Bar/Bat Mitzvah should not be the end of Torah learning. Jews have always studied Torah all their lives.

REAL LIFE

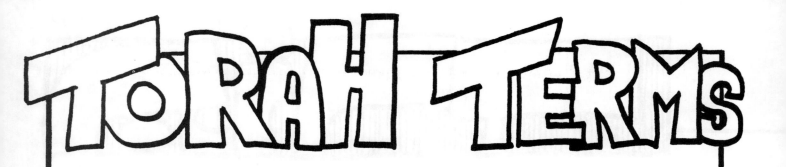

TORAH TERMS

BAR – Son

BAT – Daughter

MITZVAH – Obligation/Commandment – more than just a "good deed"

CONSECRATION – Ceremony beginning religious school

CONFIRMATION – Ceremony ending religious school

TORAH – Law or teaching

SEFER TORAH – Torah scroll (the one in the Ark)

CHUMASH – Five books of Moses (Torah in book form)

PENTATEUCH – Greek name for Chumash

MONDAY, THURSDAY – Market days (Torah is read)

SHABBAT – Torah is also read

PARASHAH – Torah portion

SEDRA – Another name for Torah portion

HAFTARAH – A reading from the Prophets or Writings

ALIYAH – The honor of being called up to the Torah

MAFTIR – One who is called to the Torah for the last aliyah and also reads the Haftarah

BA'AL KOREY – Torah Reader

BERESHEET – Genesis

SHEMOT – Exodus

VAYIKRAH – Leviticus

BAMIDBAR – Numbers

DEVARIM – Deuteronomy

SIMCHAT TORAH – Holiday when we finish and start the Torah

SHAVUOT – Holiday when God gave us the Torah

SOFER – Man who writes the Torah by hand

TROPE – Chant used for Torah and Haftarah

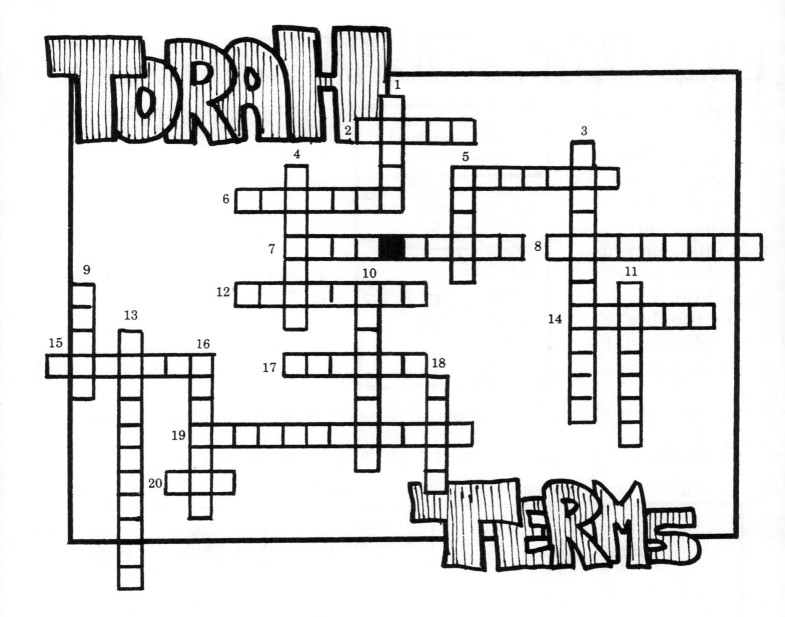

ACROSS

2. Torah writer
5. Confirmation is on _____
6. Hebrew for Pentateuch
7. Torah reader (2 words)
8. Vayikrah
12. Torah portion
14. Torah honor
15. Beresheet
17. Last aliyah
19. Celebration held on Shavuot
20. Torah means _____

DOWN

1. Five Books of Moses
3. Celebration for starting school
4. Bamidbar
5. Another name for Torah portion
9. Kids got alphabet letters covered with _____
10. Read after Torah portion
11. Obligation/Commandment
13. Devarim
16. _____ Torah (holiday)
18. Notes for Torah chanting

BAR · BAT MITZVAH THOUGHTS

Before you start this sheet, your teacher should have you list the things you think a parent should do for a child, and list the things a child should do for a parent.

At a Bar Mitzvah, a father traditionally says this blessing.

BLESSED BE HE WHO HAS FREED ME FROM THIS RESPONSIBILITY FOR MY SON'S BEHAVIOR.

QUESTIONS:

1. What is this prayer really saying? _____ _____ _____ _____

2. Do you like it? Why or why not? _____ _____ _____ _____ _____

Compare your list of parent responsibilities to this list from the *Talmud*.

A father's responsibility to his son is to...

Circumcise him

Redeem him

Teach him Torah

Find a wife for him

Teach him a craft

And some say:
Teach him to swim.

QUESTIONS:

1. Is there anything surprising about these responsibilities?
2. What responsibilities would you want to add or subtract?
3. Draw a cartoon showing a fathers responsibility to his daughter.

Bar Bo Bar Bo Bar Bat Mitzvah Bu Bu

PLANNING KIT

You have two copies of this sheet. Fill out the first by yourself, then ask your parent(s) to fill in the other. When you are all finished, share and compare the two sheets.

INVITATIONS

1. _____
2. _____
3. _____
4. _____
5. _____
6. _____
7. _____
8. _____
9. _____
10. _____

Which people are most important to you to have at your Bar/Bat Mitzvah ceremony?

PRACTICE

1. _____
2. _____
3. _____
4. _____
5. _____

What things do you need to work on before you're ready to be a Bar/Bat Mitzvah?

GIFTS

1. _____
2. _____
3. _____
4. _____
5. _____

What do you really want to gain as a result of your Bar/Bat Mitzvah?

THANK-YOU'S

1. _____
2. _____
3. _____
4. _____
5. _____
6. _____
7. _____
8. _____
9. _____
10. _____

What are the most important things for which you might say thank you?

BAR Bar Bat Bar Mitzvah Mi Mitzvah

PLANNING KIT

You have two copies of this sheet. Fill out the first by yourself, then ask your parent(s) to fill in the other. When you are all finished, share and compare the two sheets.

INVITATIONS

1. _____
2. _____
3. _____
4. _____
5. _____
6. _____
7. _____
8. _____
9. _____
10. _____

Which people are most important to you to have at your Bar/Bat Mitzvah ceremony?

PRACTICE

1. _____
2. _____
3. _____
4. _____
5. _____

What things do you need to work on before you're ready to be a Bar/Bat Mitzvah?

GIFTS

1. _____
2. _____
3. _____
4. _____
5. _____

What things do you really want to gain as a result of your Bar/Bat Mitzvah?

THANK-YOU'S

1. _____
2. _____
3. _____
4. _____
5. _____
6. _____
7. _____
8. _____
9. _____
10. _____

What are the 10 most important things for you to say thank you for?

WHAT IS AN ADULT? Bar/Bat Mitzvah was traditionally the dividing point between childhood and being an adult. Today, we may not be so sure that becoming 13 means one is an adult.

List 10 things you do now that you don't think you will do as an adult.

1. _____
2. _____
3. _____
4. _____
5. _____
6. _____
7. _____
8. _____
9. _____
10. _____

List 10 things you don't do now that you think you will do as an adult.

1. _____
2. _____
3. _____
4. _____
5. _____
6. _____
7. _____
8. _____
9. _____
10. _____

List 10 things you do now that you think you will still do as an adult.

1. _____
2. _____
3. _____
4. _____
5. _____
6. _____
7. _____
8. _____
9. _____
10. _____

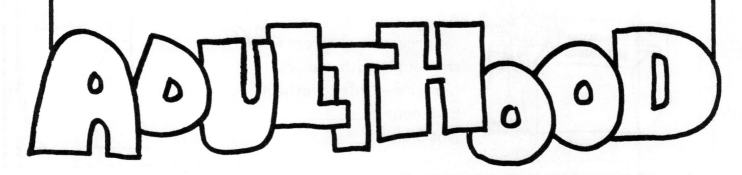

GETTING READY

These pages describe a traditional Jewish wedding. Check those parts you think most people still do today.

HAVE I GOT A MATCH FOR YOU

The **SHADCHAN** is the matchmaker. He or she helps the parents decide who their children will marry.

Still done _____
Not done _____

ENGAGEMENT

Once the parents decided that a couple was going to be married, there were lots of steps to go through.

After the **SHIDDUCH** (or match) is made, the parents sign the **TENNAIM,** the "conditions," and the bride and groom meet for the first time.

Still done _____ .
Not done _____

The **CHATAN** (groom) gives the **KALLAH** (bride) a gift or two. She gives him a **TALLIT** and a **KITTEL.**

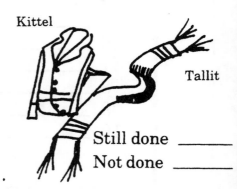

Kittel

Tallit

Still done _____
Not done _____

THE AUFRUF

On the Shabbat morning before the wedding, the Chatan is called to the Torah to show the Kallah's family how much Torah he knows.

Afterwards, the congregation showers the couple with candy (for a sweet life together).

Still done _____
Not done _____

ON THE DAY OF THE WEDDING

The Kallah and the Chatan have a mini-Yom Kippur (fast and all).

GETTING MARRIED

The wedding service has two parts:

A. Erusin or Kiddushin, which mean betrothal, and

B. Nissuin, which means marriage

BEFORE THE WEDDING SERVICE

1. The **KETUBAH** is signed and witnessed.

2. The Chatan puts the veil on the Kallah (bedeken).

A. Erusin or Kiddushin

3. They enter and stand under the chupah.

4. Birchot Erusin are said over a cup of wine.

5. The ring goes on the first finger of the bride's right hand.

SEPARATION OF THE TWO PARTS OF THE WEDDING SERVICE
B. KIDDUSHIN

6. The Ketubah is read.

7. The seven blessings (Sheva Brachot) are said. A second cup of wine is tasted.

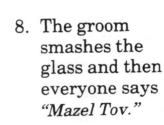

8. The groom smashes the glass and then everyone says *"Mazel Tov."*

At the meal afterwards, and traditionally at every meal for the next seven days, the Sheva Brachot are said.

WEDDING WORDS

הֲרֵי אַתְּ מְקֻדֶּשֶׁת לִי
בְּטַבַּעַת זוֹ, כְּדַת מֹשֶׁה
וְיִשְׂרָאֵל.

Be thou consecrated to me with
this ring according to the faith
of Moses and Israel. (These words make the wedding happen.)

Aufruf – Calling the groom to the Torah on the Shabbat before the wedding

Bedeken – The ceremony when the groom puts the veil on the bride

Birkat Hamazon – The grace after meals at the Seudat Mitzvah.

Chatan – Groom

Chatunah – Modern Hebrew for a wedding

Chupah – Wedding canopy (under which the wedding happens)

Erusin – Betrothal

Get – A divorce (not a necessary part of every marriage)

Kallah – Bride

Kiddushin – Betrothal (from Kadosh/Holy)

Kittel – A white robe given to the groom by the bride. He will wear it to the wedding, at every Seder and on every Yom Kippur, and he will be buried in it.

Mazel Tov – (Fill in your own definition.)

Nissuin – Hebrew for marriage ceremony

Seudat Mitzvah – Wedding feast

Shadchan – Matchmaker

Sheva Brachot – The seven blessings which are said as part of the wedding ceremony.

Shidduch – The match (engagement)

Tallit – Prayer shawl given to the groom by the bride. He will wear it daily, and at the brit of his son, and he will be buried in it.

Tennaim – Conditions (for the engagement)

FIND THE WEDDING WORDS:

Hidden in the mass of letters below are many of the wedding words from page 36. Circle all you can find.

```
K I D D U S H I N N S C I N
I C L O V E H L S H E V A H
T B T R Z B A A H M S C U T
T E N N A I M X A I E H F M
E D H U A R A T D T U A R A
L E U K R K Z A C Z D T U Z
E K C A E A O L H V A U F A
R E J L R T N L A A T N O L
U N E L L C M I N H V A H T
S B R A C H O T A L L H T O
I D C H A T A N G E T I T V
N I S S U I N C H U P A H P
O P S H I D D U C H M R A L
```

37

7 BRACHOT

1. KIDDUSH

Praised are You, Lord our God, King of the universe, who creates the fruit of the vine.

2. GOD MADE EVERYTHING

Praised are You, Lord our God, King of the universe, who creates all things for His glory.

5. JERUSALEM IS HAPPY

May Zion rejoice as her children are restored to her in joy. Praised are You, Lord, who causes Zion to rejoice at her children's return.

6. BRIDES AND GROOMS ARE HAPPY

Grant perfect joy to these loving companions, as you did to the first man and woman in the Garden of Eden. Praised are You, Lord, who makes the bride and groom happy.

A new couple is brought together with seven Brachot. These seven blessings are repeated each day for seven days following the wedding.

3. GOD MADE PEOPLE

Praised are You, Lord our God, King of the universe, Creator of people.

4. GOD MADE MAN AND WOMAN IN HIS IMAGE

Praised are You, Lord our God, King of the universe, who created man and woman in Your image, fashioning woman from man as his mate, that together they might perpetuate life. Praised are You, O Lord, Creator of people.

7. HAPPINESS

Praised are You, Lord our God, King of the universe, who created joy and gladness, bride and groom, mirth, song, delight, and rejoicing, love and harmony, peace and companionship. Lord our God, may there ever be heard in the cities of Judah and in the streets of Jerusalem, the voice of gladness and the voice of joy, the voice of groom and the voice of bride, the jubilant voices of those joined in marriage under the chupah, the voices of young people feasting and singing. Praised are You, Lord, who causes the groom to rejoice with his bride.

7·Brachot Work Sheet

Let's take a look at the way the **Sheva Brachot** are put together.

A brachah is a prayer that uses the word baruch. In the boxes on pages 38 and 39, baruch is translated as praised. Underline all the sentences that begin with Baruch.

Circle the most important word(s) in each underlined sentence.

Compare your circled word(s) with the heading for each prayer.

1. _____
2. _____
3. _____
4. _____
5. _____
6. _____
7. _____

4

A. Kiddush means _____
B. Prayers 2, 3 and 4 have _____ in common.
C. Prayers 5, 6 and 7 have _____ in common.
D. Prayers 2, 3 and 4 go from: (check one)
   ☐ general to specific ☐ specific to general.
E. Prayers 5, 6 and 7 go from: (check one)
   ☐ general to specific ☐ specific to general
F. Prayers_____and_____have two baruch sentences and both come at the _____ and _____ of a theme.
G. Prayer _____ is an introduction.

Discuss the way the Sheva Brachot are put together.

FAMILY ALBUM

Check with your parents and fill in this worksheet with pictures and descriptions of their wedding.

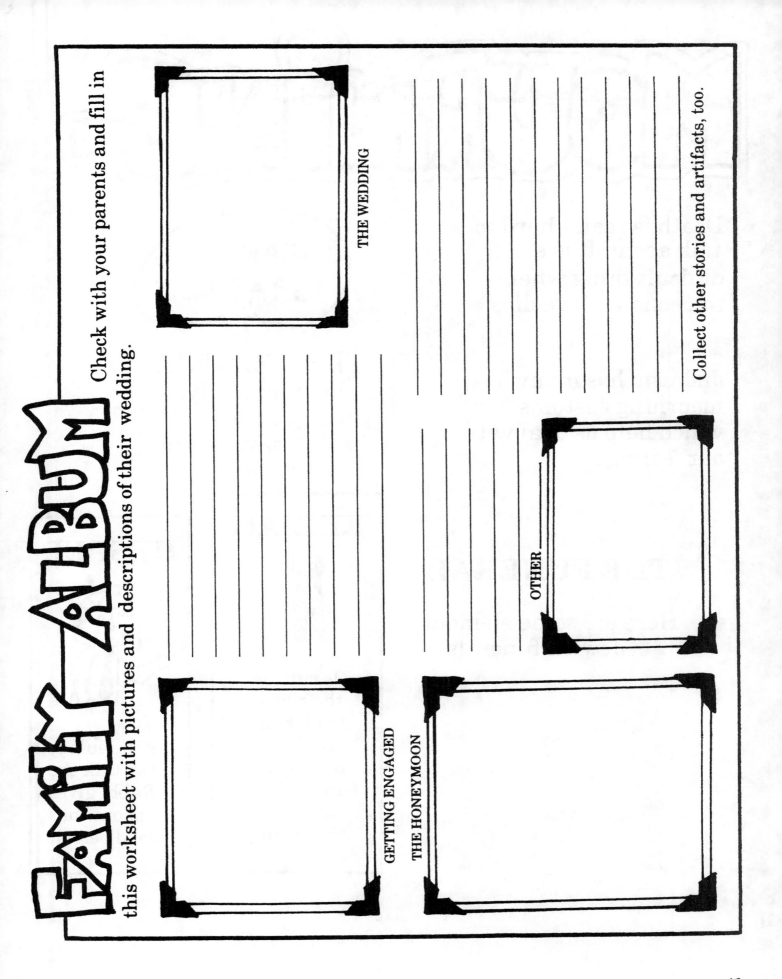

THE WEDDING

GETTING ENGAGED

THE HONEYMOON

OTHER

Collect other stories and artifacts, too.

MOURNING

Death is really hard to talk about. It is a difficult thing when someone we love dies.

Judaism has many mourning customs which help us deal with our feelings.

HEAR O ISRAEL...

THE SHEMA

Traditionally, the last words a Jew says before he/she dies.

THE FUNERAL

Here are some elements of Jewish funerals.

KERIAH

Is cutting the ribbon (which has replaced tearing the clothes) as a sign of mourning.

HESPED

is the eulogy, the talk the Rabbi gives about the dead person.

THE CHEVRAH KADISHA

The Holy Society Is a group of important people in the community who donate some of their time to perform the mitzvah of preparing the body for burial.

ONANIM

is the name given to mourners before the body is buried. Until the funeral the Onain has no responsibilities.

3 PRAYERS

EL MALAY RACHAMIM,

TZIDUK HADIN and **KADDISH** are parts of a funeral ceremony.

SEUDAT HAVRA-AH

A meal is served to the mourners on their return from the cemetery. An egg, a symbol of life, is the first thing eaten.

SHIVA

For seven days following the funeral, Jewish families sit shiva. Friends come to their home, bring them food and take care of their needs. A daily Minyan is held in the home.

SHELOSHIM

A thirty day period that follows the funeral. After shiva, mourners return to their normal lives. But they refrain from going to parties or other celebrations during the sheloshim.

SHANAH

For eleven months following the funeral, a mourner says the Kaddish daily. After that period, the family visits the cemetary and **unveils** the head stone. Each anniversary of the death is called **Yahrzeit.** Kaddish is said.

KADDISH

The Kaddish is sometimes thought of as a mourner's prayer. Let's 1) read it, 2) do the work indicated in the box, and 3) answer: What is the Kaddish about? Why is it used as a mourning prayer?

יִתְגַּדַּל וְיִתְקַדַּשׁ שְׁמֵהּ רַבָּא. בְּעָלְמָא דִּי־בְרָא
כִרְעוּתֵהּ. וְיַמְלִיךְ מַלְכוּתֵהּ. בְּחַיֵּיכוֹן וּבְיוֹמֵיכוֹן
וּבְחַיֵּי דְכָל־בֵּית יִשְׂרָאֵל. בַּעֲגָלָא וּבִזְמַן קָרִיב.
וְאִמְרוּ אָמֵן:

יְהֵא שְׁמֵהּ רַבָּא מְבָרַךְ לְעָלַם וּלְעָלְמֵי עָלְמַיָּא:

יִתְבָּרַךְ וְיִשְׁתַּבַּח וְיִתְפָּאַר וְיִתְרוֹמַם וְיִתְנַשֵּׂא
וְיִתְהַדָּר וְיִתְעַלֶּה וְיִתְהַלָּל שְׁמֵהּ דְּקוּדְשָׁא. בְּרִיךְ
הוּא. לְעֵלָּא מִן כָּל־בִּרְכָתָא וְשִׁירָתָא. תֻּשְׁבְּחָתָא
וְנֶחָמָתָא. דַּאֲמִירָן בְּעָלְמָא. וְאִמְרוּ אָמֵן:

יְהֵא שְׁלָמָא רַבָּא מִן־שְׁמַיָּא וְחַיִּים. עָלֵינוּ וְעַל־
כָּל־יִשְׂרָאֵל. וְאִמְרוּ אָמֵן:

עֹשֶׂה שָׁלוֹם בִּמְרוֹמָיו. הוּא יַעֲשֶׂה שָׁלוֹם עָלֵינוּ
וְעַל־כָּל־יִשְׂרָאֵל. וְאִמְרוּ אָמֵן:

May God's name be made great and holy throughout the world which He created according to his will; and may He rule in His kingdom in our lives, in our days, and in the life of all Israel, speedily and soon. And let us say: Amen.

May His great name be blessed forever and always.

May His holy name be blessed and exhalted, and honored, and glorified, and extolled, and magnified and lauded. Blessed be He, though He be above all blessings and hymns, praises and consolations which can be said in the world. And let us say: Amen.

May lots of peace descend from heaven with life for all of us, and all Israel. And let us say: Amen.

May He who makes peace in the heavens above, make peace for all of us, and all Israel. And let us say: Amen.

---

1. Underline every place in the Kaddish that something nice is said about God.
2. Double underline every wish in the Kaddish prayer.
3. Circle every place that mentions life.
4. Box every place that mentions death.
5. Mark ✔ the "Chorus."

MOURNING PERIODS:

Color in the periods in which these events take place:

	Between the death and the funeral	Shiva	Sheloshim	Shanah	Yahrzeit
Food is brought to the mourners					
The mourners stay at home					
Kaddish is said					
The mourner has no responsibility					
Daily minyan at home					
No parties attended					
Mourners may cry...					

QUESTION: How does the Jewish way of mourning help us deal with death?

A CONVERSATION ABOUT DEATH:

In class you are going to talk about Jewish views of death and mourning. Before the next class, ask your parents to talk about a death in your family. Write some of the answers.

1. Where were you when you heard about the death? What did you feel?

_____

_____

_____

_____

2. What do you remember about the funeral? _____

_____

_____

_____

3. What do you remember about the house of mourning? _____

_____

_____

_____

4. What do you believe about death? _____

_____

_____

_____

_____

ETHICAL WILL

A will is a document people write while they are alive which tells how things they own will be shared by friends once they are dead. Some Jews also wrote a second kind of will, an ethical will. In it they shared thoughts and suggestions for living a good life. Imagine your ethical will. List 5 of the people who are most important to you. Then list a suggestion or a wish you might want to share with each.

PEOPLE   SUGGESTION/WISH

1. _____   _____
                          _____

2. _____   _____
                          _____

3. _____   _____
                          _____

4. _____   _____
                          _____

5. _____   _____
                          _____
                          _____

ACTIVITY: Describe your feelings as you wrote this will.

_____

_____

_____

_____

VISITING A SHIVA HOUSE ...

It is a mitzvah to visit and comfort friends who are sitting shiva. While we may be a little scared, and feel that we don't really know what to say, the Jewish tradition helps us.

When we come to a house of mourning it is a mitzvah to bring some food.

You need not greet or say anything to the mourner — just being there is enough. If you have to do something, a handshake or a hug is welcome.

It is okay to be sad and cry. You don't need to cheer up the mourner. You can share the sadness.

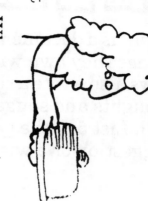

When you get to the house of mourning, the door will be open or unlocked. You don't knock or ring the bell. You just go in.

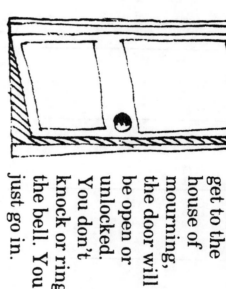

Quite often, you'll find a row of shoes outside the door. You remove yours before going in.

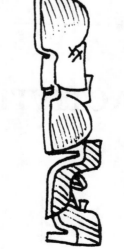

You may join in a minyan or a study session. When you leave you don't need to say good-bye. You just leave. It isn't a party and mourners aren't the hosts.

QUESTIONS

1) What do you think of these customs?

2) How do they help the mourners?

3) How do they help the visitors?

48

The Threshing Board

It used to be a custom that parents would give their children a threshing board for their wedding gift. The threshing board was used to help prepare the grain they used to make the bread they ate daily. It also became an important part of their lives. At the wedding, they danced on the threshing board. Their first evening as husband and wife, they slept together on the threshing board. Their children were brought into the world on the threshing board. A mother was delivered of her children on the threshing board. When people died, their bodies were wrapped, and they were laid to rest on the threshing board. The threshing board tied the major events in a person's life to the daily experience of eating bread. What Jewish objects work in this same way?

List some Jewish objects which are used in more than one life cycle event.

List here the places the object is used.

1. _____ _____
2. _____ _____
3. _____ _____
4. _____ _____
5. _____ _____
6. _____ _____
7. _____ _____

TiES

Let's take a second look at the ways various parts of the life cycle are tied together. This time you are going to look at themes.

TORAH – Study (Learning is a central Jewish concern.)
MITZVAH – Commandment (Jews have obligations.)
BRIT – Covenant (Jews have a deal with God.)
KEDUSHAH – Holiness (Some things and some moments are special.)

Try to find one place, thing, prayer, etc., in each step of the life cycle which deals with each of these themes. Use the chart below.

	TORAH	MITZVAH	BRIT	KEDUSHAH
BIRTH				
TORAH EVENTS Home School Consecration Bar/Bat Mitzvah Confirmation Etc.				
MARRIAGE				
DEATH				

Identify each of these items:

Pidyon Haben _____

Confirmation _____

Ketubah _____

Shiva _____

Brit Milah _____

Chupah _____

Yahrzeit _____

Match the following

BRIT MILAH	Nissuin, Sheva Brachot
BAR MITZVAH	Mohel, Sandek, K'vater
WEDDING	Blessed is he who has freed me from responsibility for my son's behavior.
FUNERAL	Shiva, Sheloshim, Shanah

List 3 life cycle events in which these are used:

Tallit _____

_____

_____

Kiddush Cup _____

_____

#7 _____

_____

EVALUATION SHEET

Complete these sentences:

1. While learning about life cycles I liked _____
_____
_____

2. While learning about life cycles I wished _____
_____
_____

3. Some questions I still have are: _____
_____
_____
_____
_____
_____

4. I'd still like to learn _____
_____
_____
_____

5. And now I feel _____
_____
_____
_____

Other comments: _____
_____
_____
_____
_____
_____
_____
_____
_____
_____